The Anointing (Pocket Size)

The Anointing (Pocket Size)

FRESH OIL OF GOD'S PRESENCE

Bill Vincent

RWG Publishing

CONTENTS

Copyright © 2020. All rights reserved.

No part of this publication may be reproduced, stored in a retrieval system, or transmitted in any way by any means, electronic, mechanical, photocopy, recording, or otherwise, without the prior permission of the author except as provided by USA copyright law.

The opinions expressed by the author are not necessarily those of Publisher.

Book design Copyright © 2020. All rights reserved.

RWG Publishing

PO Box 596

Litchfield, IL 62056

https://rwgpublishing.com/

Published in the United States of America

1

∽

The Anointing

Prayer: We need the anointing. Father, you are drawing near to hungry hearts, and your Word promises that those who hunger and thirst for righteousness will be filled. Father, we have come to this place this weekend to be freshly filled and saturated with your goodness, glory, presence, and anointing in our lives. Father, we want to encounter you. We want to see you. We want to learn from you. Father, we want to grow closer to you over these next days. And Father, I do pray that there would be a launching of a whole new season in people's lives. That Father, there will be a dramatic shift in the spirit in the lives of these loved ones of yours, and may they encounter your presence, anointing, and your life-empowering Word in Jesus' name. Amen.

Significant breakthroughs are going to happen in your life, and God is going to release prophetic keys to us that will not only release breakthroughs but also establish people in their breakthrough. I don't know about you, but I am ready for a whole new anointing, an entirely new season, a whole new manifestation of the glory of God in my life, and I know the same will happen in your life. I decree it over you from the beginning right now. Right now, you are stepping into a new place of breakthrough. You are stepping into a new anointing. You are stepping into a fresh place in God.

No matter what your life looks like at the moment or the circumstances you have, God is above it all, and you're going to get a breakthrough. I'm going to declare it again. You're going to get a breakthrough through the river of God. Are you ready for the river of God? Not only to do something in you but also to do something through you because we're going somewhere.

In Psalm 46, I want to read this and comment as we launch into this. God is our refuge and strength. I love how the Amplified Bible says it, mighty and impenetrable a very present and well-proved help in trouble. Therefore, we will not fear though the earth should change, and the mountains be shaken into the midst of the seas. Do we see anything shifting and changing in the earth today? Do we see things shaking in the earth today? Yes, there's a lot of things shaking.

There are a lot of things shifting, changing, and moving. Though its waters, and roar, though the mountains tremble at its swelling, there is a river. In other words, despite all of this, despite the shaking, the shifting, the changing, and all that's happening, we will not fear. No matter what happens around us, we will not fear. Why? Because there is a river whose streams make glad the city of God, the Holy place of the Tabernacles of the Most High. Praise God. God is in our midst, and we will not be moved. So, there's a lot of things moving around us in the earth today, but we have a prophetic promise from God.

No matter what's moving around us, God says, you will not be moved. You know why? Because there's a river and that river is going to make you happy. I said that the river is going to make you happy. And I'm going to say it until you get happy. It's one of the things I love about the river of God and the presence of God, and in His presence is the fullness of joy. What a fantastic promise that no matter what is happening around you now, you can say what is happening globally. You can say what is happening nationally. You could say what is happening locally. You could say what is happening in your home.

You could say in your family what is happening, no matter what things seem at times, it may be out of our control, in the midst of what is out of our control, there is a river on the inside of us that makes us glad, that gives us peace, that gives us joy, that causes us not to fear no matter what is going on around us. This is the launching place, and when the river is flowing, don't just stand on the riverside and watch the river flow by, jump on into it. The water is fine, jump on into everything God has for you.

I encourage you, don't miss your moment. We're consecrating ourselves; we're giving ourselves, we're giving time and energy, we're giving space to God, not just to have some meetings, but to have an encounter, to go to a new level, to get some breakthrough. So, this is where we're launching from, and prophetically, one of the things that I feel strongly in this hour and the new season that we're in, is that I don't think it's a coincidence that this weekend is Rosh Hashanah. If you're familiar with the calendars, you would have noticed that It's time for Rosh Hashanah on the Jewish calendar, which implies the head of the year. If you study that carefully, it's the head of the year as it starts the new year on the Hebraic calendar. So, I feel this is significant. As we go into this, get ready for a whole new start in your life, a whole fresh anointing.

I want to speak into this prophetic season we are in right now from Psalm 92 verse 10, it says, but my horn you have exalted like that of a wild ox. I am anointed with fresh oil, and I believe the prophetic season that we are coming into right now. This new season as things shift and come into the new, don't be surprised if God gives you a new vision. Don't be surprised if God doesn't give you some new creative ideas. Don't be surprised if God doesn't release something revived and awakened on your inside. Awakening starts on the inside; it's not just on the outside, and we're going to learn something about revival, revival is not just something you attend, revival is what you become.

There is a river on the inside, and that river is not going to stay on the inside. It is going to flow on the outside, and in this new season, there is a fresh oil that God wants to anoint you with. A fresh anointing for a new day and I thank God for every anointing we have ever experienced in our lives. I look back over my life, and I thank God for the anointing that I've experienced up to this day. I thank God for the healings we've seen, for the moves of the Holy Spirit, for the lives we have seen transformed under that anointing, but there's something on the inside of my heart that is being stirred and awakened that I know will supersede whatever oil we have experienced up till this point.

There are fresh oil and a fresh anointing for today. That no matter how great yesterday's anointing was, you cannot just coast on yesterday's anointing. There is a fresh anointing for today. There's a fresh anointing for the assignment God has for you today. Now, let me say this; I believe God is giving assignments to people. I believe God is delivering divine assignments into people's hearts. Good works prepared for them to do before the foundation of the earth. But for you to fulfill what God has for your life, you have to be anointed for it because I'll tell you this, no matter how great you are in your natural self, to achieve what God wants us to do, what's in his heart, we need the anointing on our lives.

I'll also like to say this, if you're not praying some prayers that scare you, you're not praying big enough, and if you're not praying some prayers that scare the enemy, you're also not praying big enough. Don't pray comfortable prayers. Don't dream comfortable dreams, dream something from the mind and heart of God that is so big that you wonder, God, how could I ever achieve this? That is the exact kind of dream God wants to give you. And I'm going to tell you these dreams are not just for pulpit preachers, and it's for the whole body of Christ. If that's Jesus, tell him I said, Hi. Sometimes, he calls in — fresh oil.

I want to read a scripture from Psalm 23, and these are my foundation scriptures here. In Psalm 23, I'm going to read verse 5. You prepare a table before me in the presence of my enemies. You anoint my head with oil, and my cup runs over, or my cup overflows. Again, you anoint my head with oil and my cup overflows. Can I tell you something that I love about the anointing of God? What is the anointing? The anointing is the manifest power of God that comes from the presence of God. What I love about this anointing, this oil, is that it lifts the limits off. It lifts off the natural limits. Things that we could never accomplish on our own.

God has a way through the anointing of lifting those limits off. God is not time-bound, and you know he's outside of this whole time and space thing. He's bigger than all of it. I love how the anointing can touch people right through a computer screen, months after something was recorded. That's how big God is.

That's how the anointing can operate in you and through you, and take all the limits off what you would experience in your natural self. I've experienced this in ministry where I've been put in situations where it's like, God, and there are some limits here. How do we deal with this situation? And I find myself praying a lot for different situations and sick people and all different scenarios.

That's what the anointing of God will do, and that's why I have such a conviction in my heart. God let us never, as a church, get so professional and so organized that we organize your presence right out of the church or that we organize your presence right out of our life. Do you know what I'm saying? I believe there's something about coming to God hungry and thirsty, so desperate that you surely know that you need him. That's a good place to be, knowing that you need him, knowing that you can't do it all on your own, whether it's your struggle that you're facing or the struggle another person is facing, that in and of yourself you don't have all the answers.

We know one who does have all the answers, and his name is Jesus, where nothing is impossible for him. It's a realm of glory where nothing is impossible for God. It's a realm of faith where we understand God in the natural. I got a lot of limits in my life, maybe even in myself. But God, there are no limits in you. All things are possible for you, only believe, and all things will be possible. And here it says that you anoint my head with oil and my cup runs over. There is a river, and God wants that river to overflow.

There is an anointing, and God wants that anointing to overflow. And one thing I know about the heart and nature of God that is so important is this. Have you ever taken a step back and have done this; take a step back and start to ask yourself some questions like, God, who are you? Have you ever asked that? Have you ever stopped to ponder who God is? God, who are you? Your spirit, your light, your truth, your love, who are you, God? What are you, God? How are you, God? – Trying to comprehend the invisible God. I've asked God these questions because I want to know him. I want to know him. So, I ask God, who are you? How are you? What are you, where are you at?

I ask these kinds of questions. One day, as I was pondering on this, this thought came to me from the Holy Spirit. Look at Jesus and look at the Gospels and study the life and ministry of Jesus Christ. Look at the words that he spoke, look at the actions, look at his behavior, and look at everything about Jesus. When you see Jesus, you see God. Jesus was the exact representation of the invisible God. The Bible says he spoke what he heard his Father say. He did what he saw his Father do, and his Father is the invisible God. But everything Jesus did, he did on purpose. Everything Jesus did, he did it with intention, revealing to us the nature and character of the invisible God.

So, if you've ever asked yourself these questions, who is God, what is God like, I want to know him more deeply. All you have to do is open up the gospels Matthew, Mark, Luke, and John, and start to re-read all of the life of Jesus, and you will see through every word and every action, the very nature, and character in ways of the invisible God. So, I look at this concept of God anointing us with oil and our cup overflowing.

God does not want to anoint you just so that you can
survive your life

Let me say this, God does not want to anoint you just so that you can survive your life. He anoints you so that you can thrive and overcome. And Jesus said I have come to give you life and life more abundantly until it overflows. The life of God that he's given us is not just to survive the next day. It's not just to get through our life or survive our life. This life is not meant just for survival. God wants to anoint you to the point where you are so overcoming that you wake up on Monday morning, and you have joy that you can overcome worry and anxiety, and have a heart filled with peace, that you're not dragging yourself from one day to the next. Have you ever had a day like that? We've all had survival days.

I know this is life, and I know we all go through stuff, and some days could be like that, but God doesn't want a survival day to be a survival life. He wants your overall life to be marked with his abundant life. And I think sometimes that's a choice where we choose, and we make a conscious determination. I am not going to survive my life, and I am going to maximize every day, every moment, every second that God gives me. I'm going to maximize my life. I'm going to maximize it in my relationship with him, and I'm going to maximize it in my attitude, my behavior, my thoughts, and what I choose to do with my life, I'm going to maximize it. I'm going to experience his abundant life, his joy, his peace, his anointing, and his presence that overflows.

God does not want to anoint you just for your own breakthrough

Here is another point I'll like to say about the nature of God and the anointing. This is equally very important; God does not want to anoint you just for your own breakthrough. He wants to anoint you to the point where not only do you get a breakthrough, but you are so anointed with the Holy Spirit, that there is a dimension of overflow happening in your life to where your breakthrough becomes a breakthrough for somebody else. Not just the breakthrough in you, but a breakthrough through you. God doesn't want to anoint you just for yourself.

The anointing will give you a breakthrough. It will, but God doesn't want to anoint you just for your own breakthrough. He wants you to come into this dimension of what we call overflow. So that not only are we getting healed and free, and are we getting whatever it is that we need from God in our soul and our mind and our body, whatever it is that we need from God. I know a lot of times; people are motivated to draw near to God because of their need. But at some point, it has to become bigger than our needs. We know God loves us, he cares about us, he's going to help us, and he's going to strengthen us.

He's going to help us overcome and be healed and be whole on the inside, but it doesn't end there. God is not a God of just enough. He's a God of more than enough, and we need to get a revelation of this aspect of the heart and nature and character of God that he is not a God of just enough. He is a God of more than enough. Sometimes, we have to hear it a few times, not just enough. When we have a vision of God, where he's a God of just enough, then our faith is God anoint me or help me so that I can get what I need and get my breakthrough or get my healing or get my freedom. Just enough, God, just enough anointing from God to survive this day or just enough anointing from God to get over this struggle or overcome this temptation. Just enough, anointing.

God doesn't want to give you just enough. He wants to give you more than enough of his anointing in your life. How do I know this? Well, I look at the life of Jesus. Do you remember when there were 5,000 men, not including women and children, probably 15,000 people and the disciples were like Jesus, send these people away, there are too many of them we can't feed them, all the need is too great, send them away from Jesus. And Jesus turns to them, and he said, feed them. In their minds, they see their limitations, and they're saying send them away.

It's impossible, and Jesus is like, feed them. Here are all of the grown-up disciples, all thinking, what is he saying? Then in the middle of all that, there's a little boy that comes forward with some loaves and fishes, a little boy. Now, just making a note of this in the Bible, Jesus never calls us his adults. He always calls us his children. So, no matter how old we get, we are never too grown up to be God's adult, we are always as children. And here was a little boy that had a faith that was like, Jesus. I know this doesn't look like much, but here if it helps, it is, and he gives Jesus the few loaves and few fishes, and Jesus takes it, and we know what he does.

Number one, he thanks God for it. Number two, he blesses it, and then number three, he breaks it and puts little pieces in all the hands of the disciples. Imagine this picture. All the grown-up disciples are sitting there with a little piece of fish and bread in their hand, and they're looking down, and I'm sure there were, at least, one of those disciples that thought to himself, lunch, for me, just enough for me. All you people go away, and this is just enough for me. I'm sure one of them thought it, and then Jesus turns to them after he's put it all in their hands, he says turn around and start to give it away, and I'm sure as they were moving, they were like, this is going to be gone real fast.

No miracle had happened yet, no sign, no wonder, but as they take what's in their hand and start to give it to the next person, in that moment of action, a miracle goes into action. Suddenly, what's in their hand starts multiplying, and somewhere along the way, the multiplication happened to the degree where they could no longer hold in their hands what started in their hand and they had to get baskets, and by the time fifteen thousand (15,000) people were fed, there were twelve baskets full. Now, if God were a God of just enough when that last person was fed, the multiplication would have stopped, and there would have been nothing left over if he was a God of just enough.

In this illustration of Jesus, in this divine miracle encounter, at the end of everyone being fed, there are twelve baskets full leftover, one for each disciple telling me the heart and nature of God that he is a God of more than enough, not just enough, but more than enough. Sometimes, we come to God with our life. I don't know if you've done this, I have done this before. I come to God with my little life, and I say, God, here's my little life.

Here's whatever strength I think I have. Here's all the weaknesses I have, and I put it in your hand, God. And you see when you put even what looks like a little or in the natural, it looks insignificant.

You put it in the hands of God. He has a way of taking that and multiplying it to the point where the impact released through your life ends up being way more than what it started with in the natural. We are to give our lives to God, saying, God, here's my life. Here are my strengths; here are my weaknesses, and here's my availability. Here is my free will of what I choose to do with my life. Here's the provision of my life. Here are the giftings of my life. Here's everything God. You put it in the hands of God, and a supernatural multiplication of more than enough starts to happen.

It's like you can't give away everything you have and when the anointing of God touches it, and the faith of God is in your heart because you have a revelation of the nature of God. Having a revelation of the heart of God is what gives you faith, and when you have faith, that's when the impossible becomes possible. That's when the little becomes multiplied, and that's when the overflow happens. Overflow, everyone says overflow. My cup runs over. I really believe that God wants to saturate us with his presence so this weekend, that we become so saturated with God, that everywhere we go, we overflow this anointing, this life, this provision, this healing, this breakthrough and this freedom that is on the inside of us to other people around us.

Do you know what I have discovered? Sometimes, things happen at the same time. And I wish I could say I passed every test. I wish I could say I was like Paul and Silas, just praising God in prison. Sometimes, I haven't passed the test, but I'll tell you I learned this lesson.

Let's get so filled with God that we shock people with his love and his goodness everywhere we go. Such that they get shocked into the revelation of who God is by overflow. By being so full that everywhere we go that river that makes glad the city of God, that that river is overflowing out of us and touching the people around us. Oh, praise the Lord. This is what we were all destined for. This is what we were created for; to be living, walking, breathing representatives of the invisible God because he's in us, and he flows and overflows through us.

There is a presence we carry as Christians. Sometimes, we don't even know that we carry God's presence because we get so distracted with other stuff. We get so distracted with stress and things. Have you ever gotten distracted with something causing you stress, and at that moment, you're not like, Oh, I feel the glory. Instead, you're like, ah, I want to kill someone. Do you know what I mean? It's like you feel the stress of situations or circumstances. You're not necessarily floating in the glory at that moment, but God is in you. He's always in you by the Holy Spirit. He's in you.

He anoints you with the oil of joy. He anoints you with fresh oil, and that overflows from you. God has called you to be a kingdom influencer. That everywhere you go, you influence people with the life of God, the presence of God, the joy of God, the peace of God, and the anointing of God. I believe you can be so saturated with God that your whole house gets anointed. Your home gets anointed that when people walk into your home, they walk into the presence of God. I say, let that be our goal that we cultivate so much of the presence of God in our lives, that when people come near us or even in our homes, that they walk right into the presence of God.

You can cultivate the anointing in your home. Praise God. You can cultivate the anointing in you and your home so that when people come in, they get free and get healed. Praise God.

It's time for the Church to grow in hunger for a fresh anointing of God. May the Lord bless you and keep you in your pursuit of Him.

About the Author

Bill Vincent is no stranger to understanding the power of God. Not only has he spent over twenty years as a Minister with a strong prophetic anointing, but he is now also an Apostle and Author with Revival Waves of Glory Ministries.

Bill offers a wide range of writings and teachings from deliverance, to experiencing the presence of God and developing Apostolic cutting edge Church structure and drawing on the power of the Holy Spirit through years of experience in Revival and Spiritual Sensitivity. Now, Bill focuses mainly on pursuing the Presence of God and maintaining Revival.

His over 50 books and still counting has since helped many people to overcome the spirits and curses of Satan.

Recommended Books

By Bill Vincent
Overcoming Obstacles
Glory: Pursuing God's Presence
Defeating the Demonic Realm
Increasing Your Prophetic Gift
Increase Your Anointing
Keys to Receiving Your Miracle
The Supernatural Realm
Waves of Revival
Increase of Revelation and Restoration
The Resurrection Power of God
Discerning Your Call of God
Apostolic Breakthrough
Glory: Increasing God's Presence
Love is Waiting – Don't Let Love Pass You
By
The Healing Power of God
Glory: Expanding God's Presence
Receiving Personal Prophecy
Signs and Wonders

Signs and Wonders Revelations
Children Stories
The Rapture
The Secret Place of God's Power
Building a Prototype Church
The breakthrough of Spiritual Strongholds
Glory: Revival Presence of God
Overcoming the Power of Lust
Glory: Kingdom Presence of God
Transitioning to the Prototype Church
The Stronghold of Jezebel
Healing After Divorce
A Closer Relationship With God
Cover Up and Save Yourself
Desperate for God's Presence
The War for Spiritual Battles
Spiritual Leadership
Global Warning
Millions of Churches
Destroying the Jezebel Spirit
Awakening of Miracles
Deception and Consequences Revealed
Are You a Follower of Christ
Don't Let the Enemy Steal from You!
A Godly Shaking
The Unsearchable Riches of Christ

Heaven's Court System
Satan's Open Doors
Armed for Battle
The Wrestler
Spiritual Warfare: Complete Collection
Growing In the Prophetic
Faith
The Angry Fighter's Story
Understanding Heaven's Court System
Restoration of the Soul
Spiritual Warfare Made Simple
Aligning With God's Promises
Deep Hunger
Beginning the Courts of Heaven
Breaking Curses
Writing and Publishing a Book
How to Write a Book

Web Site:
www.revivalwavesofgloryministries.com

www.ingramcontent.com/pod-product-compliance
Lightning Source LLC
LaVergne TN
LVHW051516170726
843492LV00002B/966